AF261061

Venetia

Kirsty Jean

Text, illustrations and photography © 2019 Kirsty Jean, all rights reserved

No part of this publication may be reproduced
in any form or by any means without the prior written
consent of the publisher, excepting brief quotes used in reviews

Credits to the contributors
— Leesa Davis, Sharon Wilkosz and Zoe Garner for editing and proof reading

Kirsty Jean

Follow me for updates and more of my projects
@kirstyjeanwrites

Printed in Australia

First Printing: 18th November 2019
ISBN: 978-1-64713-027-5

In loving memory of Leesa Davis—

For my mum
I never would of survived without you
I am honoured and blessed that you got to read my first book
Everything I write in the future is for you
With your endless love guiding me
you're my one and only
I love you
always

"No one else knew. It was almost like I tired to erase it from my brain.
And when it finally came out, it was like a big, ugly monster.
And you have to face the monster to heal."
- Lady Gaga

The substance of Venetia is made up of seven

Listen

Body

Stone

Soft

Hands

Substance

Complete

Complete -

adjective

having all the necessary or appropriate parts
(often used for emphasis) to the greatest extent or degree, total

verb

finish making or doing
provide with the items necessary to make something full or entire

Listen

1st October 2018

I could no longer find comfort in the words and pages of others
so to survive I made my own

1st November 2018

I am cursed with the knowledge of others
This is a power I have been entrusted

— that I don't think i want, lonely it can be

29th August 2018

I was trying to disappear
everything was too loud
i started to dig a hole too retreat
you all watched confused but to busy to ask why
it was okay watching
but when I started too bury myself
it was easier to cover the hole and not water the seed

i had to wait for the rain.. in a drought

12th February 2018

I'm still me
I'm in here somewhere
I locked myself away
deciding it was safer being locked inside the sadness

playing games of hide and seek from my own mind

30th August 2018

Libra—

No one can break my heart the way you can

Only your person is capable of that

29th September 2018

Lightning struck in Venice
sending us into a new cycle
our heads spinning — we thought it was the wine

27th September 2018

I have been through the worst horrors

None of them broke me to the point where I don't know myself

where i can't feel myself

Not even depression made me feel this empty

3rd May 2018

Stop feeding their ego
watch their power disappear
yours will soar

1st October 2018

The problem wasn't that I couldn't find my people

I couldn't focus on people. period.
I made no sense to people.
People made no sense to me.

28th August 2018

Don't get soul mate confused with illusion

28th September 2017

the hardest part about becoming who you are, isn't hurting other people

— it's staying in your magic when they finally see it

30th August 2018

It is not the world that is dark
It is us and we don't deserve her

20th May 2018

How can I expect the truth from others

When I can't even expect the truth from myself ?

Don't let someone's bad experiences
be the reason you are okay with the way that they treat you

You deserve so much more than you are okay with
I wish you would allow yourself to see it

17th August 2018

Prince charming kissed sleeping beauty and saved her life...

I was awoken by a kiss also...
he was no prince charming only a demon hiding behind lost brown eyes

2nd September 2018

You are about to regret the moment you saw me as vulnerable, as weak
as less than
I was asleep
I was a little drunk
I was in the safety of my friend's home
What you did took away parts of myself I feared would never return
Which makes us both wrong about something... both because of your actions
Yours was seeing women as less than and for the taking
How dare you be rejected by two?
How dare you think that the rejection of two women gives you the validation
the go ahead to rape one of them?
Your mistake lies all over this whole thing

You saw me as less than, weak, as vulnerable

Do I seem like any of those things to you now?
I never was.
Even while you raped me.

You believe or have been lead to believe women are these things
Well I just shared with the world that you raped me...
How weak do you look now?
How lesser than?
But more importantly... How vulnerable do you feel right now?

15th February 2018

The greatest pleasure in life is having the courage and bravery
to believe in yourself enough to do the things
that people tell you that you can not do.

16th April 2018

The greatest pleasure in life is having the courage and bravery
to believe in yourself enough to do the things
that others make you feel that you can not do.

19th May 2018

I made the inside of this house beautiful again—
i invited you all to see but none of you care
you'll all care again when the outside looks "beautiful" again too

———————

I told me—
you'd only come back when the outside looked beautiful
i was hoping you'd prove me wrong

24th September 2018

We promised forever and a day
I needed a minute to love myself
I'm still sorry, i had to steal some time to save myself
so that forever would see another day

31st August 2018

You always get three wishes
But sometimes you have to ask for one more
That's the name of the game

(I asked for you- yet I still never saw you coming)

27th August 2018

Sunflower —

I see you sunflower
so thin you might blow over in the wind
begging me to come in
fix all these things you just can't make feel right
your head is going to have to hang for a little while more sorry sunflower

love the sun

5th May 2018

You've taught me only how to fear
Men's faces scare me
I never know who i'm going to get

every time i love they mirror something that is you or relates

The fog is a trick
It's black and brown
But it smells of roses

10th October 2018

Just because they didn't believe you
doesn't mean that someone else won't

— this is the most important thing to remember

remember everyone has their option
their own problems
which hurts more than any other pain i have experienced
when you need love the most

don't take someone's word by law
because you need it the most right now
more than anything else
sometimes even the people whose job it is to protect you
make you feel safe — fail you. Don't stay.

Always go find someone that believes you
always go find someone that protects you
if ever you need reminding of your worth and truth
read this as a reminder
that i believe you
that i will always send love to you
when you need love more than anything else

1st November 2018

I have never told a man what to do with his body
apart from one - I begged you to stop trying to rape me

you didn't listen

26th August 2018

As i told her what he did to me she held all of me in her hands
telling me with her eyes that she was never going to let me go
i could finally see the green light
breath re-entering my lungs
someone was finally listening - safe

Body

12th February 2018

I'm still me
even after what you did
ripping my soul to shreds
he saw that broken ness in me that you left behind
he thought we were the same you see

broken together perhaps
even when I screamed no, he heard convince me
you had branded me
convince me —
i need validation prove that I am worthy of attention
this is not the attention that i had held as a label about my head
especially considering i lay asleep asking for nothing but rest

9th May 2018

I flinch when you touch me
I fear it is him

28th August 2018

He touched both my arms my feminine and masculine

everything that i had still frozen inside of me
he reset me
just for one night
to show me what we could be
if i let it all unfreeze
if i let it all heal

14th September 2018

You took all my freedom
From everything i lost this was the worst

it ties into everything else

5th May 2018

I know my own body so well at this point
I wonder if anyone else could play it right

9th September 2018

you are not an if

i do not wonder if you will ever kiss me
i do not wonder if you will love me
i wonder when — when will you hold me, be soft with me

(make no mistake practising patience is exhausting)

30th August 2018

You are all the things i think about wanting in someone to love

But he makes me smile so hard i have to close my eyes
i clench all my body inwards
i curl my toes
i bite my lip
i draw my breath
i feel the shivers overtaking my body
i hold my face in my hands

and all he's done is enter my mind

— you used to be all the things I think about wanting
in someone to love

29th May 2018

I forgot my power
after you messed around my petals — trying to take me as your own
you forgot i was a rose until I cut you with my thorns

you can't take things just because you want them
she didn't want you
I am not extra space for you to fill that void with
I needed support instead you came and took the very little I had left

1st September 2018

Families feel like trying to draw the perfect circle
they go around and around

drawing the perfect one is impossible

13th March 2018

I know you love me
yet you only say it when you feel us to break again
i can't live off that anymore
i need you to show me or I need you to go away

4th July 2018

You took me prisoner inside my own body
I am still trying to work out how to <u>not</u> want to try and escape

28th September 2018

You were always there
i just couldn't make you out through the fog

12th September 2018

I'm clinging on to the last pieces
i feel so suffocated
that the people i cling onto
suffocate under what you did to me too

16th October 2018

I saw you preparing to go under
four trips around the sun
this is how long we have to be under reconstruction
i can feel my heart ready to chime again
i have to wait for them
i'll be there when you chime again
welcoming me back to my new home

26th June 2018

His burden is that he made you choose
Your burden is that choice
My burden is that you choose him

— You choose your rapist friend over your raped friend

9th May 2018

You won't have sex with me
you know I want to make love
you won't do it
you know we could never just be sex
you are unsure if you are ready to make love again

— be soft with me i won't hurt your heart like they did

23rd May 2018

To all the boys
who wouldn't have sex with me
because i was too desperate
— thank you

You taught me how to hold value in myself

The difference between sexual chase
and your sick game
of me getting validation in you finally touching me

—

But also fuck you for playing that sick game
I don't actually have thanks for any of you.

Thank you, to the boys that only came to chase

6th September 2018

Most days it's hard to find the worry to shower
I'm dealing with feelings i pray you never have to
I'm learning to live with them
You can live with my leg hair

14th April 2018

I miss those two girls
they were so close to it
We are crushing because we were so close to it
that intoxicating energy
that pure magic of being yourself
you got scared and i of losing you
now here we are

20th June 2018

You think it was hard to be my friend?
Think about how hard it was to live as me
Then try telling me how hard it was to be my friend again

28th September 2018

"You respect my opinion as i respect yours"

No.
I don't. neither do you.
My rape is not an opinion.
it happened.
there isn't a debut

he raped me— you believe me
yes or no.

Fear convinced me to stay safe
in the boredom
slowly becoming the person
I worked too hard to move away from

13th September 2018

I've never had sex
I've been raped

17th September 2018

if you wake up
and they are touching you
— it's rape
I don't care if it's your boyfriend or husband.
Girlfriend or wife.
You were asleep ...
they didn't start touching you because you made them wet
they started touching you
because you were seen as vulnerable because

you were asleep

26th September 2018

My darling you need to be your own north star

Stone

2nd September 2018

I was always able to make people smile and laugh
my darkest moments
were not being capable
of even understanding how I used to do that

1st September 2018

Attack — Secondhand

Men realise it's actually not about you
So when you feel "attacked"
please understand
i didn't say stop raping us
in consideration of you
i want men to stop raping women
if you don't rape women don't get offended —
be offended that you're in a minority that rapes 1 in 5 women

stop trapping us inside a box we have no say over
use your voice
understand i feel attacked every second of every day
that i walk this earth because of men
understand that when you feel attacked

— that is me crying out for help
but you feel attacked

3rd October 2018

I loved you because you were the only boy
at the time that sort of made me feel safe
you knew this and you used it to stop me from leaving

— illusion

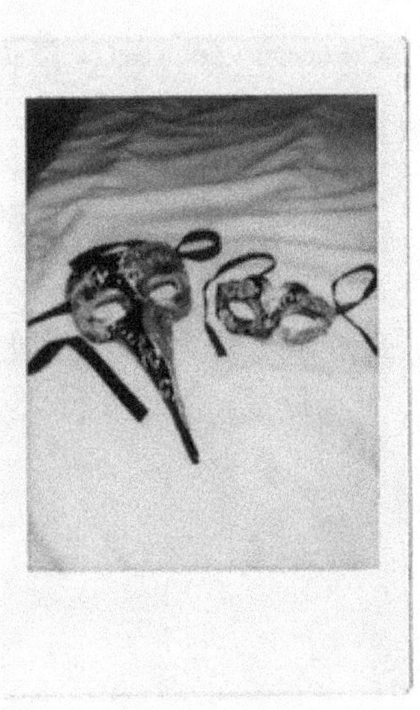

10th May 2018

I moved heaven and earth for you
what we need is to raise hell... together.

1st September 2018

She was warmer than sunshine
one day you will realise what you threw away
it will be after your ego is crushed
those muscles turn to fat
— things of fake substance always deflate in the end
you can't cheat happiness
it will always leave you
along with the fake substance
- in time

24th September 2018

You knew I wasn't myself
Still you left me
Why because I told you I didn't know why I don't trust you ?

Well how am I ever meant to trust you again after this.

24th August 2018

Cancer —

you're about as sweet as vinegar
but you taste like truffle

5th May 2018

The love you offer is the curliest kind — you're here but you're not
until the noise we make to fill the silences becomes too much for you
you shame us for craving your love

"Go where your heart sends you"

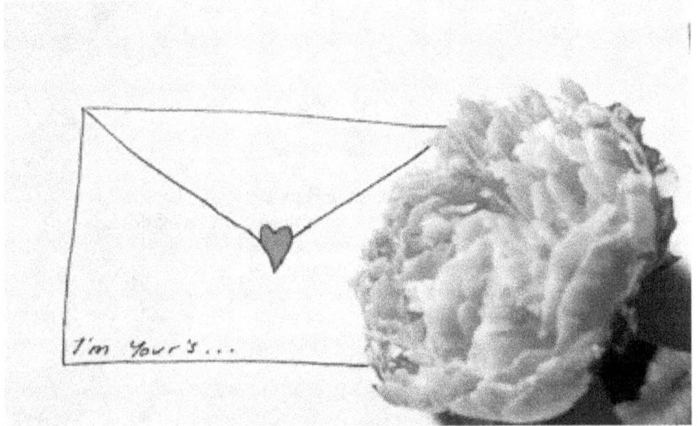

Mine keeps re-sending me back to you

12th February 2018

I haven't seen you in a month
so when i finally did i thought i would be excited
instead i got scared
hide behind my fear
now i will probably never seen you again

13th September 2017

This is one of the most beautiful things i've ever seen
Yet I don't even know who created it

3rd May 2018

We are one of the most beautiful messes I've ever seen
I finally know who created it

30th August 2018

I'm so scared to lose you that i don't even tell you that i want you

I don't have you
every other time I've opened my heart for someone
that makes me feel the things that you do
they don't just break my heart
i trust you
i know you would only break my heart

it's not you i don't trust
it's the past
i hate that it makes me doubt you

I'm so scared to lose you
yet i can't wait to have you
never before has someone made those two things
inviting together

1st November 2018

I might of loved illusions
which made me scared to love you
thinking that it might be the same
truth is no one has ever made me feel the things that you do
you make me feel the sort of things everyone dreams about
little do they know are so rare
their illusion tricks them into thinking they have found it

I'm not scared that you will break my heart
I beg you to try

12th September 2018

I want you back in my life
but i am so angry
because every time i try to reconnect — all i hear is

you dropped me like it was nothing
the moment i wasn't there to help your ever beck and call anymore

31st August 2018

I used to let you get away with everything
because i love you

that is not love
that is you taking away my power
because you don't know how to keep your own

i will always keep giving because i love you

1st September 2018

Because I will always keep giving
i have stayed away
for the first time i couldn't choose you over me
if i did that would be the end of me
in turn would be the end of you

14th October 2018

The smoke comforts me through my second panic attack
my love (illusion) at the time
taught me to smoke as a way to calm the panic driven itch
— smoke was my friend

Now — the smoke is no friend it made the fog thicker
pulling me backwards

29th September 2018

I used to get hurt by your lack of appreciation of what
i mean to you

now i see it's not like that at all
— it's somewhere between lack of energy from adopting into
what they all want you to be and that you don't hide around me

I'm the only one that really sees you

24th September 2018

I ignored your anger as i told you my story
so you could see why i left
because for once it needed to only be about me
forgetting the impossibility of that
we are one trying to function in two bodies, hearts and soul

12th February 2018

The outcome is not always clear
it could be a gamble
you might feel it is worth your sacrifice
get over the other side and realise — it is worthless

it is worthless now
it was worthless then
this is life's game — you just see the difference now

30th August 2018

Mother earth and the human race
are a perfect example of how man appreciates women

12th September 2018

I keep thinking it is you that should be worried about me
that i would be breaking your heart
that i would be the one needing saving
i'm now starting to wonder
that i've been looking through rose coloured glass
it is i that would be saving you

— i don't want to be saved or to save

i want to be soft, i can be soft with him

i'm sorry, i didn't mean to break your heart

12th September 2018

he always had my heart.

20th May 2018

My own mind is holding me from the answers I seek

27th August 2018

You're pulling me
my mind is already foggy
now you two are pulling at me

27th August 2018

Cancer —

i stay away determined to not get my toes wet
before i even realise you've pulled me into the deepest depths

i'm not scarred
i'm excited
i want to see more

— i'm scared of hurting you

27th August 2018

Virgo —

I sit by the window
watching the snow fall
you take me away from everything
it always comes back to you

all the different snow flakes can flirt with me
i don't see them — the only one I'm looking for is you

9th May 2018

Your hands shake
your breath draws
you're so angry your sister worries for your life
she worries your heart will fail you
i wonder if your heart will finally breakdown
you're scared you cant find your way back to us

break- let yourself crumble.
those walls you're hiding behind that you built to protect us.
we don't live behind them anymore...
neither should you

12th September 2018

She brought back the light

she raised her magic hands
i cried —please don't take anything off me
that will stop me from writing
she replied —my love i can't take which belongs to you
i only take which does not

— she showed me the path back to my magic

20th May 2018

How can i expect the truth from others
When i can't even expect the truth from myself

23st September 2018

Invading —

You don't like someone invading your space being emotional or physical
— does that make you uncomfortable

sex is intimate
opening yourself up
vulnerable at times

Being raped is someone
invading your intimacy and vulnerability
without being offered a visitor pass

16th July 2018

There is my truth
There is his truth
There is the truth

Regardless of the story teller
the truth is you had sex with me even though i told you no
So in my truth and the truth that makes you a rapist
I wonder what you make of your truth
— I'll ask you next time i see you
you don't scare me anymore

I know you are scared of me
you never show up when you know I'm invited

You should be scared.

25th September 2018

The universe

I'm not going to promise you they won't leave
The only way I will <u>ever</u> leave you is if i have no other choice
But i will always choose to find my way back to you
You are part of the balance between my sun and moon
I had to learn to be my own north star again
I never wanted to leave you
— half my struggle came from understanding that i had to

5th September 2018

Humans destroy that which they do not understand
So of course we are all out to destroy ourselves

16th July 2018

You need to think about that you will be ruining his life —
I won't be ruining his life-
he ruined his life when he decided that it was okay to rape me
That was his choice
He took my choice away
He branded himself with that label by committing the act
I will be doing nothing but speaking the truth

4th September 2018

I'm almost over the rainbow
I didn't leave you behind
One of us had to make the leap first
It had to be me
You couldn't even watch me jump

Soft

5th December 2017

I felt you in my dream last night
I woke because you squeezed my hand so hard
At first i thought it was magic, then realised it was real
I felt you longing for me

19th January 2018

I felt you in my dream last night
I woke because you squeezed my hand so tight
At first i thought it was a dream
—then realised it was magic, it was real
i felt you long for me

21st September 2017

I'm not going to ruin myself in the hope that it might save you.
I love myself enough to know that now.

13th April 2018

I'm not going to let you make me think
I need to ruin myself to save you
I love myself enough to not let that happen now
I'm also not going to save you
I'm going to stand beside you as you save yourself

12th February 2018

Love is not meant to be a sacrifice that hurts
you are doing something for the person you love
if you feel
that it costs you even the smallest part of yourself walk away
a sacrifice is not brave
unless the outcome is greater then the cost

there is nothing that should cost more to you
in your life
then yourself

23rd May 2018

After we met everything unfroze all at once —
it kept us apart

i know we have a story that wants to be told
when we met even fate's heart quickened

9th May 2018

Father I barely even know where to begin

1st October 2018

Travel always guides me to the truth
it unlocks my deepest wounds
my harshest truths
without travel my heart would not soar
my soul would lay empty for more taking

28th September 2018

I see you all but you're the only one in focus
i see you sunflower

12th February 2018

I saw me —
when i yelled at you all
you saw me, really saw me
it was scary - i liked it
barely any of you could look at me
i'd been suffocating me
for so long to make things comfortable for you all
that when you pushed me it bent apart of me way too far
this was the bounce back

14th September 2018

For the first time in the history of our friendship
I chose myself
You've punished me for it ever since

12th August 2017

I might not love you like I did.
But you still glimmer in some of the things I see

28th September 2018

The insects and reptiles are at war around me
fighting over the flowers

12th February 2018

I'm still me ...

Who is me?
have i even seen her?
has anyone?

why does she hide her beauty away
from a world that is in such desperate need
of such beauty
a refreshing breath of chilling, un-nerving air

you all need un-nerving....
probably even more so than i do

23rd May 2018

I hope your heart takes it's chance to have a story with mine

23rd May 2018

The boy under the tree that saw what i really needed — a cuddle and a cry
you touched my heart
you helped rebuild my soul

10th June 2018

I asked you to touch my lips
i asked you to touch my neck
i begged you to touch my petals

— you were the first boy to truly listen
you gave me what i needed not what i wanted
you touched my heart

16th April 2018

For all of twelve hours -
You cared more about my life
then anyone else in it at present

I would of kissed you, I know you would of kissed me too.

Because you asked the questions I had been waiting to hear.

We both knew exactly what this was.

We were both a reminder
for the other of that each of us had once forgot.

—

For me you were a reminder of how to be soft around others

I don't know what I was for you.
But that wasn't my job I was something for you, not something for me.

—

I think about if we will ever meet again

The warmth between us is the stuff they write songs about.

—

But I'd hate to see you and you make me feel like stone.
I'd hate for you to see me and our twelve hours turn to stone.

19th May 2018

Under the stars of Venice
You appeared from nowhere
You pressed your lips to mine
The pressure of you on my lips
awoke a part of me I always try to hide.

You're electric —
But you'll never be mine

10th September 2018

I just broke your soul telling you how he broke mine
But we took the first step towards finally being able to heal

8th September 2018

I thought I was getting you out of here so you could see the world

Now I see that you needed to see a world not around me

The blood of life
The blood of rebirth
The blood is cleansing
The blood is pure power
The blood dripping from my holy womb

9th September 2018

Pink and yellow rain drops
This is how I began to heal—
my hands could barely hold together
from their overwhelming power
They crave them
I can't decide if I chose them or if they chose me
I needed them but they wanted me
My hands are finally coming back to me
No matter what you took from me
I'm going to get it all back
and more
But I'm not going to steal it
I'm going to earn it
Giving fills the soul
with an energy
that i wear on my fingers

16th July 2018

It feels like being on a plane that's never going to land
Where no one wants to talk to you

5th September 2018

This isn't a story where one chapter
comes along ruins the overall story
simply
because they didn't want to read the whole book

This is the type of story
where that person turns into a cliff note

19th of April 2018

You softened instantly
for a moment and only slightly

Hands

12th February 2018

Over —

You think i am not over you?

i look into your face
i stay where i am
I am so steady that I can't even remember
how it feels to be in love with you

5th September 2018

She held the world in her hands
Gold pouring out of them
Accepting through writing — learning to heal

30th August 2018

No matter how horrible "the world" is to you
every night before you rest your eyes
ask yourself were you kind?
so you leave this world kinder then you found it

17th July 2018

People have forgotten how to listen
Once i have healed
I am going to focus on learning how to listen again
People don't need you to fix them—
they just need you to listen

16th April 2018

I belong in London
My soul is from Venice
My heart was gifted to me from Paris
My hands have been many places and held many stories

11th October 2017

Soft as a petal and sweet as honey.
She lay her head down at peace with herself
and dreamt of the world

19th May 2018

Her petals softer then before
and her words as sweet as they were bitter.
She lay her head down at war with the world
and dreamt of herself

Austria —

12th August 2017

i held myself together
until i got to my room
i let only two tears fall
then reminded myself you're not someone to waste tears on

26th August 2018

What you did was not worth my tears
who you are is worth them all

13th September 2018

I miss you —
I know I seem angry
I am
Not at you
It's misplaced
I can't throw it at him for what he did to me
So i've been stabbing it at people i love
Truth is what I really feel towards you is
Sadness
I miss you
Then i remember how we got here
I get angry
I throw it at you

25th September 2018

I can feel myself again
I wonder where i go when i feel empty
I am scared of the emptiness
I love when I feel whole
I don't know how to enjoy myself without worrying
when I'm going to leave again

16th July 2018

Who broke you so badly that you look
at a drunk asleep girl
and think it's okay to
rape me?

3rd September 2018

I read my poems back
The dates saying one thing
My mind was telling me another

Safety in denial

13th October 2018

For the twenty second time on the thirteenth day the sun rose
completing another year around the sun

2nd October 2018

The worst thing you took from me was my hope
it shook me to my core
being the one thing
i always believed to be stronger than fear
Where do you find hope after being raped ?
You can always find it in love
Lucky for me i was surrounded
Some people just lay it on you
Some don't get why you need hope again
hopefully they still lay love on you
even when it doesn't feel like it

Don't mistake their lack of understanding
for lack of love
Don't mistake their love
as understanding

10th October 2018

Why don't women come forward —

'Women come forward
tell us your tales of pain and trauma
we will hold you, my arms are open.'
-we believe some of you
-we believe you sort of

Women don't come forward
because the fear of being told their trauma didn't happen
is in many ways worse then the act itself
My sexual trauma <u>therapist</u> told me -
i can't say i was raped because i don't remember

i don't remember the physical violet act
there is a lot i do remember
i left my body to protect myself
as he started to rape me
my mind protected me
in a way that you in your paying job
failed me

I was bleeding after
I was in physical pain
I was in shock after to the point of not being able to sleep
I was incapable of letting anyone touch me (even now)
I was overcome with ptsd, depression and anxiety after

(this is the short list of who i became after i was raped)

I might not have remembered straight away
but that is called science
I was told to trust in people —
they will believe you
How are we meant to trust
when someone whose job it is to believe me
to help me
told me — it wasn't rape

28th September 2018

Cloudy night —

I thought the worst of this was over
that you raping me
was going to be the worst you could do to me
you are the reptile that raped me
leaving me in a puddle of ptsd—
let me just add you to the list of men
that have tried and failed to extinguish the fire in me

i am not my own weakness
she is my weak spot
she is who i love most in this world
yet she can barely be around me
as she still tries to block the event from her mind
the event of you raping me
My fear
Did you make the most important person in my life
witness it
Finding me after was enough
but because she is the most important person in my life
all i can think is thank god you chose me
i think you should thank god you chose me as well
i wouldn't have frozen the same way
I did if you had tried to rape her
i honestly have no limit of what i might of done to you
or maybe
you should have just chosen not to rape
either of us...
but you did.
so perhaps you should pray to god rather
than thank her
the hell we are going to raise upon you—
only she can protect you from.

2nd October 2018

My body became an enemy
i'm permanently attached to
I have hated my body
I have never felt like a stranger
inside of my physical home
You made the place
that should be the most familiar place in the universe
the most itchy and achy
space to date i've been forced to
existed in

12th February 2018

Growing the flowers was easy
keeping them alive was the hard part
the garden we had grown together was beautiful —
finally a team

it had felt like magic
only now do i realise that it was
we worked so hard to get there
watching our garden die ripped me to bits...
leaving holes in my soul

13th October 2018

I promised I would never leave you
I will spend the rest of my life trying to make up
the time i had to steal from us

1st October 2018

I couldn't bare to look at any of my sunflowers
Not when I can't be their sun
The sun was burnt out
the stars followed quickly
after leaving everything to survive in the darkness
It's selfish but i couldn't bare
not to see their heads raised
warm smiles when it felt like it was my fault
that this wasn't the case
I'm sorry that he took away all the energy
in this universes solar system
i know it wasn't my fault
what he did to me
but i feel at fault for what it makes me
do to you

11th September 2018

We both tried to complete to bloom
into what we aren't sunflower
Thats why our garden almost died

November 2017

"he"

He took my heart
He took my voice
He took my body
He took my soul
He took my mind
— after he took my heart
because i had already given him everything else

They took it all
but the worst thing that he took was my hands
Without my hand
i lose the power to reconnect
to every other part of myself

Heart —
You broke one before
At least i thought you had
You were all that stayed in tact
I hide you in plain site, yet not even i could see you
Once i finally found you — you were still so whole and pure
Glimmering, almost taunting me to let you break...
Well you got your wish then didn't you.

I saw you, i reached
you came as soon as you were called
But you broke as soon as you lay in my hands
It only made sense - everything else was broken too
You were the last to break but the first to rebuild
Not because it was easy
but because that is what hearts are designed to do
You fell back together
like you had done it a million times before
— every other part of me followed in time
Slowly you helped as i put myself back together again
It didn't take you long to give yourself away again
Sometimes i wonder why i even call you mine
You might be my heart
but you always seem to belong to someone else

Voice —

He, she, they.
took my voice.
The first time i was told to be quiet
because i was being "too bossy"
the first time i was told to sit down and listen
- someone more important is speaking
the first time i was told i couldn't read that book
— it was for boys
the first...
the first...
the first...

I stopped and just let them take it
It was easier, to just hand you over.
No one would bother me, if I just kept you quiet

But then when i got drunk, you would lose yourself
Scream words that you don't mean
at least you were saying something
shaking afterwards
what had i just done
well let me tell you
i knew they wouldn't listen
— they like you silent and in pain
but you just throw those painful thoughts
at the only one who actually listened
with intent to wound.

Body —

I was barely breathing
Wounded so badly
— i still don't understand how i survived
we locked eyes
when our mutual friend brought you over as a surprise
You had a warm smile and lost brown eyes
You ignored me
pretending you were wherever she was instead all night
The sun kissed the ocean
The moon danced in the night
We all drank until even the moon grew tired
I bid it and you all goodnight

My arm tingled as you rubbed it
Had you finally left her and come back to me ?
No.
Those aren't your lips
that definitely isn't your touch
Stop it every part of me begs
Who is touching me
I turn my body away
again he plays with my skin
I lay as still as i can
maybe he will stop
He grabs my arms
Lays me flat on my back
He's laying on top of me now
I can almost make him out in the darkness
It definitely isn't you
The realisation of what is happening takes place
A single tear falls
I hide it by turning pillow to face
He forces his lips to mine again
They don't taste like yours no matter how hard i try
I think of your soft touch
silk lips
your warm smile
You're not actually here, you're with her
I think of your eyes, so whole and dear
They feel like home
His are lost and brown.

Soul —

Many chipped it before you
Until six single words shattered me whole
You didn't even say them
You had someone else say them

— someone else had to tell me what you should of
You left me for her
at the time i thought — I hope she's worth it
Five years later.. I know she isn't she's horrible to you
You still message me, just in case
Even though you won't let yourself think it
You know it - I still feel like home
You message me even more now that I'm whole.

You liked when I wasn't because I was broken
waiting
Yet you still called me home
I let you go
looked inside someone else to fill the last of the gaps
It wasn't easy putting myself right with you
both holding onto me so tight

I'm whole now
He likes me that way
Didn't fix me
He just enjoys me
Doesn't need me
- love doesn't actually work that way
I offered you both my soul, not my heart
You crushed it
- it felt like i was laying under shattered glass
So weak that every time
i tried to put myself back the same
— i shattered into a million more
Until I realised what you both had done

Substance

13th March 2018

I gave you a glimmer of substance and you soften instantly

1st September 2018

He is the first soul
that i have loved that mirrors the kind of person i want to be—
rather than the person i am trying to grow out of

1st October 2018

Rob him right back —

That thing he did to you
he robbed you of a million things
one of them being your choice
that defines you until you choose
choose to not let it be anything to you
you choose to take your choice back
let that define you

your choose to let his choice to take yours away
make it mean nothing more than
his weakness to understand the enormity of your power

13th September 2018

I broke my own heart — she cried
No you saved it — I replied

15th October 2018

When they say follow your heart —
it sounds like it should take you to the happy ending

you followed — it hurt like hell
your heart led you where you need to go
not where you wanted

it will, sometimes your heart takes you to some dark places
to remind you why you want the light
so bad in the first place

28th September 2018

All the different flowers i care and nurture
i welcomed into my life — the warmth and joy their energy holds
the hurricane destroyed the land and the flowers trust in the world
an unforgiving and violent energy

1st October 2018

The smoke curls its way up through my nose
The panic rises in me it brings it all back
The smoke makes its way through my body as the panic rises
The smoke used to be my friend
The smoke brings it all crushing back to me

the rape
the panic

the cigarette smoke i'm breathing in so deep
as my last hope
of riding out this hurricane
he threw me into
that just keeps sucking me back in

24th September 2018

Days bleed into years
then one day the curse you placed on me
was challenged by a beautiful soul
he didn't come to lift the curse

— he was sent to remind me that i could

3rd October 2017

Very quickly you are going to be alone
and only then will you actually look at yourself
because of who you think you are

— you will think it is too late

29th September 2018

This year she didn't feel like going to the ball
she felt like waiting for the sun to shine
so she could dance in a green field
wearing a dress made of flowers

20th July 2018

I saw the flowers, a yellow glow
Pulling me towards you

26th September 2018

I had to choose what was vital for my survival
You didn't make the cut
Not because you aren't crucial to my existence
But because the only thing on that list was my existence

1st August 2018

Twin Flame —

I can't - i cried out
you can
it hurts too much
thats exactly
why you must keep writing my love

— i can't see you
I hear you when i need you
I feel you burning through every word
that pours from within me

25th September 2018

Please understand that I will always
have time, space and energy for you

But I still need to heal
from being abandoned by you
more times then I choose to count

29th September 2018

Funny enough i wasn't thinking about ruining his life
(because apparently he's ruined mine)

i was more concerned about making sure he doesn't attack anyone else
like he attacked me
you are very un-educated, naive and blind
on the topic of rape

— so understand your opinion is not only unwanted...
its also invalid

10th June 2018

I'm scared that we are just another sick game
My head worries what you'll do to my heart
You don't make me feel that way though
It feels like you got under my skin
trying to run with the pulse in my veins

i don't need you to see me
i want to see you though, all of you
the more i see the softer i become
yet it's like we are both too scared to actually look
it makes me really sad
why wont we just look

2nd September 2018

You look at me like I'm your favourite book
that you just can't stop reading
But you haven't read me complete once yet

I found them, the extra pages I've been searching for
Can we please read them together
I'm scared of why they have been so hard to find

29th September 2018

a reminder —
when you yourself don't know what you like
it is impossible for others

26th September 2018

You are the sun
She is the moon

I am the universe
you're both currently allowed to exist in

I am scared of being empty
of being nothing
I crave substance

29th September 2018

The story is complete at least to my satisfaction

23rd September 2018

I floated on the water finally relaxing into the way it moved me

The white roses blooming could finally begin

1st November 2018

I forgot how fucking powerful I actually am —
I took it all back
My energy is massive
If you were someone that tried to take it from me

I would watch your back

Complete

1st September 2018

Complete poems —

I've been looking for all the pieces of the puzzle, looking through fog
i finally managed to find them all now
nce i put them all together.. you're screwed — everyone will know what you are now

(if you're reading this i put them all together - and now they all know)

11th September 2018

You tried to be a rose
Sunflowers always follow the sun
Follow my light sunflower I'll guide you home

14th April 2018

I think of how light I was while on that floating city.
I feel the substance that became me.

21st May 2018

I think of how light I was while on that floating city
Finally understanding the substance inside of me

21st October 2018

All last night did was highlight
how far I've still got to go rather then how far I've come

1st November 2018

Don't bully yourself my darling
just because someone else did...

—she didn't have far to go at all truth be told.

13th September 2018

There is no trick to healing

Somehow you just find yourself in all the mess

the tip-
is to look
hold yourself in love
i promise you're there

19th May 2018

How do i accept this?

it's apart of who you are now
You accept this by accepting yourself

11th September 2018

If you ever doubt my love
While I put myself back together
after what he did
One of my first thoughts was I'm glad it was me and not them

28th September 2018

Suddenly all the fog lifted
this time for good
finally this cycle was over
she breathed in the blossoming air
it had got better
she had made it over the rainbow

15th October 2018

Angels look after us
Angels need to be looked after too

29th September 2018

She tries to understand who you are
what you did
by dating other men like you

I worked out what you did — the type of man you are
No one else is going to tell her, all but me that is

I won't let her throw away
her chance at pure love
trying to work out the mysteries of a broken man

13th September 2018

I've been waiting for you
I look at her
I know that smile
I haven't seen that glimmer in her eyes in years
The warmth of her magic fills her cheeks
Her laugh echoes over her face
I've missed you
— I whisper as i finally
see myself again in the mirror
I catch the tears filled with happiness
in my hands
that found the magic that finally overflows again

19th September 2018

Trust —

She listened as my sun and moon
made their way back to balance again

I wait for the day her balance
gets thrown back into the hurricane
I promise to hold you the way you held me
I promise to listen the way you listened to me
I promised to stand by your side
while your sun and moon relive the hurricane

12th February 2018

When we met— you were like the sun and i the moon
me feeding off the extraordinary light you radiate
i still want to be like the sun and moon
i want to shine of my own first
working together
— so say goodnight to the world and everything it has to say
kiss me and we'll dance around in the stars

12th September 2018

I look at myself in the mirror and watch the tears fall
— how do i heal
my darling no one can do it for you
special loves are a part of the healing
but they do not have the power to heal you
that comes from within and blooms outwards
start with your root
ground yourself once more
that is how you become complete
but first complete the poems

29th September 2018

I'm sorry if my opinion on my rape offends you
i just thought you ought to know?

1st September 2018

Virgo —

You did something i feared impossible
You made winter turn to spring

October 7th -

It's been one year since we met
It's been one year since you unfroze it all
It's been one year but I'm healing
It's been over a year since this all began to unfold
It's time for a new dawn to rise

Hand in hand —

27th July 2018

Stop looking for me in everyone else
look into my eyes again
i know it's scary but they hold the truth

So you have to choose
look for me in everyone you meet until
your last breath ... or finally breathe again

28th September 2018

You are my perfect mirror
i didn't understand what that truly meant until now
I've looked into your eyes, i can finally breath again
take my hand so we can take back the world

28th September 2018

I wasn't angry with you
however that didn't stop me throwing it at you

I break only by confusion of how you could keep leaving me
— why won't you help me

Then all at once it all fit together
i had mourned myself after he raped me
I need to mourn you
what he has also done to you
The second hand trauma you felt through me
I can still feel the fear in your eyes from when you found me
it still haunts me

i have to mourn what he's done to us

1st October 2018

In the forest maze we lay
A moment frozen in time
The stars hold protector over a glimpse of the future

3rd October 2018

Beeeeeeeeeeeeeee me
Beeeeeeeeeeeeee me
Beeeeeeeeeeeee me
Beeeeeeeeeeee me
Beeeeeeeeeee me
Beeeeeeeeee me
Beeeeeeeee me
Beeeeeeee me
Beeeeeee me
Beeeeee me
Beeeee me
Beeee me
Beee me
Bee me

Believe in yourself again

1st November 2018

If you think my words are too bold
My energy too fearless...

Honey this is me barely even getting started....

3rd October 2018

You look around and the new spring blossoms all around- healed

Healing happens in whatever way it wants to
One second you're soft
One second you're stone
One second you're a million exploding stars at once
Then after what feels like a forever of seconds
the day comes,
the healing is complete

The complete poems.

1st November 2018

Venetia flooded releasing ten years of withheld magic

1st November 2018

Then just like that
she remembered how to listen
she lay at peace with her body
she had built a back bone made of stone
she let her heart be soft again
she let the magic pour from her hands
she overflowed in substance
she was complete

cherry blossoms pouring from her soul

Dear reader,

I wrote Venetia solely for myself, the idea of publishing never crossing my mind.
I was in desperate need of healing,
so I began by doing the one thing that feels most natural to me.
I wrote.

Venetia is a female name meaning Venice.
While visiting Venice I ended up in this little store that only sold hand made items.
We were looking for post cards, when I found her.
I have always had an obsession with journals but I had never seen any as beautiful.
Her leather body, thick blank pages, detailed front cover, a bubble around Venice,
the last page marked "handmade in Venice."
Venetia - her name hovering above the city,
waiting for me to wonder what her name meant.

I bought her and shortly after started pouring myself into her pages.
A raw, messy and detailed depiction of living with PTSD.
Struggling to understand relationships.
Rebuilding a relationship with one's self.

My biggest lesson being loving yourself comes easy,
its other people that make it messy.
You just love them anyway.

I have chosen to share her in the hope she might help or hold others,
in the way she did me.
This chapter is the hurt and I do not hold back in what the hurt entailed.
Always keeping the same goal in mind throughout my journey, to be soft.
Which is what I hope you find in your journey.

Always, Kirsty Jean

www.ingramcontent.com/pod-product-compliance
Lightning Source LLC
Chambersburg PA
CBHW061504050726
47593CB00002B/438